For Mom ~

*who insisted I stay in the kitchen with her and "keep stirring."
There were so many other things I would have rather been
doing. But I stirred.*

I didn't know that she was preparing me for success.

She did.

PIE TOWN PIES

Making pies with the Pie Lady of Pie Town

Kathy R. Knapp

Kindle Direct Publishing

CONTENTS

Pie Town's History

Pie Town Cafe & Hotel, circa 1927
Photo by Russell Lee, courtesy of Library of Congress

A Texan named Clyde Norman came to New Mexico seeking gold in 1922. Land in this area was up for grabs to anyone who could 'prove it up' by living on it for five years or more. Mr. Norman filed a mining claim called Hound Pup Lode on the south side of highway 60, a two-lane dirt road used mostly for cattle drives. His land was located near the Continental Divide with beautiful views either direction.

Needing cash to subsidize his operation, he began supplying travelers with gas, kerosene, snacks and sundries which he purchased in Datil, 22 miles away. He built a store near his claim and called it 'Norman's Place.'

Clyde fondly remembered his mother's blue-ribbon winning apple pies and started making them to sell, as well. People all over Catron county started talking about 'Norman's pies' so he decided to replace his sign with one that read, **'PIE TOWN.'**

Harmon Craig arrived in the area in 1924. Harmon and Clyde became mining partners and Harmon's wife and daughter took over the pie baking business. Soon more people came, seeking refuge from the Great Depression. They built log homes, dug wells and planted crops, entitling them to become landowners, too.

Seeing this growth, Harmon applied for a post office. The government replied: "Pie Town is a ridiculous name, beneath the dignity of the postal department, pick a real name." But Harmon would not budge and Pie Town was granted a post office in 1927.

Homesteading couldn't have been easy but it must have been one heck of an adventure for those hardy souls looking to remake themselves with very little except ingenuity and the human spirit to survive. Oh, and pie.

The Thunderbird Trading Post becomes the Pie-O-Neer

The Thunderbird Trading Post was built in 1945 as a respite for travelers driving long stretches of highway 60. This lone structure situated on the crest of the Continental Divide appears as a mirage on the horizon when seen from a distance. The silhouette of an iconic Thunderbird catches your eye as you get closer, its bold block letters imploring you to **STOP**. Wide wooden steps invite you to step back in time. Welcome to the wild wild west!

My family discovered this trading post fifty years later while on a road trip through New Mexico in the summer of 1995. Our destination was the Very Large Array (VLA), a radio telescope observatory located on the plains of San Agustin, near the village of Magdalena. This installation receives and analyzes radio waves from space and was featured in the movie **CONTACT** starring Jodi Foster.

While driving, we saw a road sign for **PIE TOWN**, 45 miles past the VLA. Everyone agreed that we should go for pie after we toured the array. *This is what Road Trips are all about!* When we got to Pie Town we found the trading post...defunct. Weeds were the only thing prospering here. A sign on the door said, **'For Sale.'**

Dissapointed, we sat in our car wondering what to do. We could see lights through the screen door so we ventured inside. An elderly couple watched us as we rummaged through dusty yellowed postcards. My curious mother asked the couple why there was no pie. With a reply as dry as his personality, the old man stated, "too much work."

We bought a few momentos and then drove back to our base camp. My mother, who had baked many a pie in my grandmother's cafe in Illinois, grumbled about how wrong it was that you couldn't get a piece of pie in Pie Town. I heard her say, to no one in particular, "If that was *my* pie shop..."

There's no more pie in Pie Town.

When we got back to Dallas we couldn't forget that sad trading post with no pie. My then-husband Thomas Hripko, a talented writer and musician, wrote a bluesy ballad about Pie Town's plight called 'No More Pie In Pie Town.' One day he broached the subject of buying the building. We called my mother in California and she jumped at the opportunity to *put the pie back in Pie Town.* She rented a U-Haul truck and packed it with all of her furniture, ready to move to New Mexico. There was just one problem: finding the money.

A pie shop in Pie Town?

Bankers in Dallas ushered us out of their glitzy high-rise offices, trying not to laugh. In their defense, it was hard to find a map that showed Pie Town really existed. Finally, a third-generation banker from the historic town of Socorro, New Mexico got it. He remembered going to Pie Town for pie when he was a child; a loan was granted.

Thomas and I made many trips from Dallas to Pie Town to help my mom ready the facility. Being a novice photographer, I eagerly documented this experience, as well as everything else in Pie Town. It was obvious that many of the original buildings - and some of the residents - were not going to be around long. I envisioned a gift shop that would feature my photographs, along with locally made Native American jewelry, pottery and rugs.

My mother needed a helper but there were no candidates in Pie Town. My daughter, Wendi Rae, who was in Chicago taking a gap year before college, happily signed up for the job. Thomas engaged us in a naming project. There were some quirky suggestions like 'Crazy Mary's' but it was ultimately decided that we would be called what we were... modern-day Pie-O-Neers!

It took a vast amount of elbow grease to get the place ready but we finally had our Grand Opening on November 11, 1995. Just in time for Thanksgiving, Pie Town would once again have pie!

Three generations of pie bakers, Veterans Day 1995

Slowly people came, curious neighbors and the occasional tourist. At that time most travelers preferred to drive on the interstates, uncertain of services on backroads. One day I had an idea. I would get mom to bake a few extra pies and I would take them to Visitor's Centers with our business card and this message:

'There is once again pie in Pie Town.'

My mother did go crazy, but in a good way. Her menu included breakfast, lunch and dinner, a daily Blue Plate Special, and pie, *seven days a week*. It wasn't long before the ranchers were regulars. I loved hearing the jingle of the metal spurs on their boots when they walked through the door. Crews of working cowboys gathered around the long wooden table next to the woodstove, drinking bottomless cups of coffee and eating biscuits and gravy. My mother was in her element.

Curve Ball.

About a year later Mom started having a hard time breathing. Worried, I came to stay with her and insisted that she see a doctor. The diagnosis was emphysema, undiscovered until she moved to 8,000 feet. The doctor prescibed oxygen and an immediate move back to lower elevation.

What now?

My stubborn mother refused to leave, hoping the oxygen would be enough. As I watched her health continue to decline I put my foot down and tearfully sent her back to California. We were all devastated.

Without mom our options were limited. We could try to sell the place. Or, I could make a major life change and try to fill some really big shoes. By then the place had gotten under my skin.

What I lacked in experience I made up for in desire.

My daughter and I decided to try to keep the doors open, uncertain but determined. We put mom's phone number on speed dial and racked up some enormous long distance bills, this was pre-cell phones! Her patient instructions and loving encouragement saw us through the rough transition. At times the shop would get really busy and kind neighbors would show up to help. Everybody pitched in and did something and then everyone got pie. I think they enjoyed being part of the chaos. I know they enjoyed the pie.

Mom was never able to come back but I sent her every article about the pie shop; the walls of her home were full of our awards. When she passed away in 2013, she knew that we had, indeed, *put the pie back in Pie Town.*

Mom in the old pie kitchen, 1996.

You Do The Math

The mathematical constant Pi is an irrational number that begins with the digits 3.14. On Pi Day, March 14, completely rational math teachers and students faithfully drive from Socorro (90 miles away) to Pie Town for a piece of pie. Pie fanatics from near and far join in the annual celebration.

A pie pilgrimage of sorts.

For that reason, March 14 was the day we always reopened after our winter hiatus. It was a great way to start our season and reconnect with everyone.

Seanna, John, Me, Jenny, Stanley, Virginia & Tanya
3.14.20

The Pie-O-Neer was the place to be in Pie Town on Pi Day.

But this year was different. It was 2020. The pandemic was out there but it hadn't gotten here, yet. Many customers had preordered pies so we pushed aside nagging uncertainly and kept baking. We set up a sanitizing station at the front door, keeping the acrid smell of rubbing alcohol far away from the pies. For one day we would not fear the unknown, choosing instead to embrace the familiar comfort of friends. When the last slice of pie was gone I posted pictures of the day's festivities on Facebook, adding that we would evaluate the situation and reopen in a couple of weeks.

Weeks turned into months.

By summer we knew Covid-19 was here to stay. Our self-service Pi Bar 'pie-ateria' would not comply with new safety regulations so we remained closed, trying to visualize the future. We reasoned that after 25 years we had made *enough* pies. Our operation had outlasted even the Oprah Show!

We put the pie shop on the market for sale.

It seemed like everyone wanted to move to Pie Town and become a pie baker. We interviewed hopeful candidates for over a year but Pie Town is not for everyone.

Then fate intervened.

A chance encounter with the woman who was operating another shop in town brought a surprise ending to our search. Sarah Chavez, a relative newcomer to Pie Town but not to the food business, was exactly what I had been manifesting...a 20-year younger version of ME!

Sarah Chavez, the NEW Pie Lady of Pie Town!

As soon as I met Sarah I immediately recognized the same nurturing spirit and unwavering drive that my mother had possessed, essential requirements for this job. We struck up a friendship... and a deal.

Sarah puts the 'H' in Hospitality and I know she'll honor my mother's traditions, but in her own unique style.

Kathy Knapp and Sarah Chavez
2021

It's Your Pie

For years I've been handing out recipes. *These* recipes. The ones we made in the pie shop regularly. They are easy to follow and don't require hard-to-find ingredients or technical cooking skills. Pie, to me, should be simple. And fun!

Crimping the crust

These recipes are merely foundations. They worked for us. Once you know the basic steps required, experiment and make them with ingredients that you like or have available. Make the pie yours. After all, it literally bears *your* fingerprints.

And don't forget the most important ingredient: LOVE!

PIE

Ice water. Two silver knives to work through the flour and shortening, add salt. It is an old art. Do not work late into the night, with sleep nipping at your sleeves, you will fall off, wake up at three a.m. to a room full of smoke, two black disks in the oven, bad smell. Do not think about business, or the wave of darkness spreading through the Arts, do not think about depression looming on the horizon or the rhetoric and nonsense our leaders toss into its mouth, or the prospect of revolution in America. Zen. Concentrate on the art of pie. It is an old art. Ingredients spread through the house like a layer of snow, later people say: O, Pie. Pie. We love pie. It is a good art. No one will say, Make this pie with only one silver knife, or no ice, or make it with chalk instead of flour. Fill the pie with ingredients at hand, cans of things, fresh fruit, cheese. Add it to a feast. Eat leftovers for breakfast the next day, the celebration begins again, pie filling the recesses of the body, exhilaration. Pie, it is an old art. If we lose it, infants will wither in their mothers' stomachs, writhe at sunken nipples, men will lose direction, US Steel will manufacture rubber and the pillars of society will flop around like spangles on a half-mast flag. Pie. The planets are lined up -- Saturn, Uranus, Mars, Jupiter pull earthquakes, pull poison from beneath the surface. Pie, cut through the mix gently, roll out on a layer of wood and flour, pie. Flute the edges, pour in apples and cinnamon and spices. Pie. Zen. Concentrate on the art of pie. The rites of passage pull us through the gates of depression and war. We shall make pie. Cannot resist. We shall celebrate Christmas, Thanksgiving, the Fourth of July; holidays shall find us traversing the continent in search of heritage. No one makes pie like Mother does. Pie. No one says one pie should represent all pies. Pie is like a thumb print. Some are sour. Pie is silent, making only a light simmering noise as it bakes in the oven. It spreads scent gently into our hearts. There is ceremony as pie is lifted out of the heat. They gather. O, Pie. The clutter is swept away, space around pie is brought to sharp focus. Light pours down on pie. Concentrate. The art of pie is an old one. Try to imagine life without it. Like the unveiling of a great painting, breaking a champagne bottle over the bow of a ship going off to sea, the ceremony as a cornerstone is laid, pie. Do not roll the crust too thick, roll gently or the center will unfurl, rub extra flour on the rolling pin every fourth stroke, remember these things. Create pie often so the art is not lost. Do not forget temperature. Cold is essential, then heat. You must have an oven, cannot make pie over an open fire or in a barbecue pit. Be firm with those who insist pie can be made in a crockpot or on the back window ledge of a Pontiac left out in August sunlight. Respect the rules of pie.

PERMISSION TO REPRINT "PIE" BY SUSAN BRIGHT FROM TIRADES AND EVIDENCE OF GRACE, 1992, IS GIVEN BY PLAIN VIEW PRESS, AUSTIN, TX

PIE CRUST

PIE-O-NEER PIE CRUST

Gramma Rosie's NEVER FAIL Pie Crust Recipe

Makes 5 Crusts

5 cups all-purpose flour
1 cup cold butter (2 sticks), cut into small cubes
*5 ounces lard or shortening
1 teaspoon salt
1/2 teaspoon baking powder
1 egg
1 teaspoon apple cider vinegar or white vinegar
Ice cold water to make 1 cup
*If using all butter (instead of half lard or shortening) *almost* double the amount of butter: 1-1/2 to 1-3/4 cups.

In a large bowl sift together flour, baking powder and salt. Using a pastry blender, two knives, your fingers or even a food processor (but *only* on pulse setting) first cut in/ incorporate butter without smashing it into too small of pieces, and then cut in/incorporate shortening/lard until mixture roughly resembles coarse sand with small lumps of butter remaining visible.

Break an egg into a liquid measuring cup. Add vinegar to egg, then add ice cold water to make one cup. Beat slightly with a fork. Slowly add liquid mixture to dry ingredients - a little at a time - integrating lightly with large fork (like a salad fork) or your hands until dry ingredients are moistened enough to hold together. You may not need all the water, but you may need to add a little more. Add just enough to make it coalesce. Scrape the bottom of the bowl as you work to ensure all dry ingredients are being incorporated.

Without overworking the dough, take about one-fifth at a time and gently form into 'snowballs' in your hand; don't compact it. On a lightly floured surface, gently shape balls into disks (like thick hamburger patties). It may take some patience to convince them to stay together. Gently transfer the disks into an airtight plastic bag and chill for 20 minutes to an hour. Dough disks can be rolled at this point or frozen in airtight bags for later use.

It's Just How We Roll

Hint ~ Every day pie crust varies; if mixture seems too dry to hold the shape of a ball, add a little more water, but don't add too much at a time.

This is YOUR creation, have fun with it.

WHOLE WHEAT PIE CRUST

*For a more hearty flavor try using this whole
wheat flour/all butter version*

Makes 2 pie crusts

1 1/4 cups white whole wheat pastry flour
1 cup whole wheat flour or white flour
1/2 cup (1 stick) cold butter
1/2 teaspoon salt
1/4 teaspoon baking powder
1/4 to 1/3 cup ice cold water (about 6 tablespoons)
1/4 teaspoon apple cider vinegar
1 egg

In a large bowl sift together flour, baking powder and salt.
Using a pastry blender, two knives, your fingers or even a food

processor (but *only* on pulse setting) cut in/incorporate butter without smashing it into too small of pieces. Mixture should roughly resemble coarse sand with small lumps of butter remaining visible.

Break an egg into a liquid measuring cup. Add vinegar to egg then add ice cold water. Beat slightly with a fork.

Slowly add liquid mixture to dry ingredients - a little at a time - integrating lightly with large fork (like a salad fork) or your hands until dry ingredients are moistened enough to hold together. You may not need all the water, but you may need to add a little more. Add just enough to make it coalesce. Scrape the bottom of the bowl as you work to ensure all dry ingredients are being incorporated.

Without overworking the dough, take one-half at a time and gently form into 'snowballs' in your hand; don't compact it. On a lightly floured surface, gently shape balls into disks (like thick hamburger patties). It may take some patience to convince them to stay together. Gently transfer the disks into an airtight plastic bag and chill for 20 minutes to an hour. Dough disks can be rolled at this point or frozen in airtight bags for later use.

Hint ~ Every day pie crust varies; if mixture seems too dry to hold the shape of a ball, add a little more water, but don't add too much at a time. TRUST YOUR INSTINCTS AND KEEP TRYING!

HOW TO PREBAKE A PIE CRUST aka Blind Baking

For crusts that are filled with custards & creams

Pastry for a single crust pie

Preheat oven to 400 degrees F.

To prebake pie crust:

Using a fork, liberally prick bottom and sides of a cold unbaked pastry in a pie pan. Line pastry with aluminum foil or parchment paper then fill with pie weights or beans, almost to top of rim.

Bake in hot oven (400 degrees) for approximately 15 minutes. Carefully remove weights and foil or paper. Reduce temperature to 300 degrees and continue baking empty pastry shell another 15 minutes or until nicely browned all over. No tacky spots should remain. Cool on wire rack then fill with your favorite things.

GRAHAM CRACKER CRUST

Sometimes you want a little something different; this is great for fluffy fillings!

1 sleeve graham crackers, crushed (1-1/4 cups)
1/4 cup sugar
4 tablespoons butter, melted

In a small bowl, mix together crumbs, sugar and butter. Press mixture into a 9" pie pan. Put in freezer to chill well before filling, or bake at 300 degrees for 15 minutes. Cool before using.

OUR REGIONAL
SPECIALTIES

New Mexico Apple w/Green Chiles & Pine Nuts

Chocolate Chess w/Red Chile Powder & Walnuts

Southwestern Peach w/Red Chiles

'Hearts on Fire' Cherry w/Red Chile Powder

NEW MEXICO APPLE PIE w/ GREEN CHILES & PINE NUTS

The pie that bites back!

Makes 1 pie

Pastry for a double crust pie

6 to 7 medium apples, peeled, cored and sliced (we use half Granny Smith tart and half red sweet - any kind except Red Delicious)
2 tablespoons lemon juice
1/2 cup sugar
1 tablespoon cornstarch or tapioca starch
2 tablespoons cinnamon, plus scant for decorating
1/2 cup pine nuts, toasted
1/2 cup medium green chiles, roasted, chopped and drained

(more if mild, less if hot)
1 tablespoon butter, cubed
Egg white beaten with 1 tablespoon water, for glaze
Decorative sugar, like demerara or crystals, optional

Preheat oven to 425 degrees F.

Place apple slices in a medium bowl and splash with lemon juice.

In a small bowl mix together the sugar, thickener and cinnamon. Sprinkle the mixture over the apples and mix to evenly coat. Add pine nuts and chiles and mix again.

Fit one layer of pastry in the bottom of a pie pan, gently tucking it in along the sides so there is no space between the pastry and the pan. Using kitchen shears or a paring knife, trim overhanging edges of crust to about an inch beyond the edge of the pie pan. Save scraps to make decorative chiles.

Fill with apple mixture, mounding in center. Dot apples with butter.

Using a pastry brush, glaze the outer rim of the bottom pastry layer with the egg wash mixture. Place the top pastry layer over the apples. Trim the overhanging top pastry layer to slightly longer length than the bottom layer. Gently press the two layers together to make a seal all around the perimeter of the pie. Lift the overhanging edge of the sealed pastry up slightly and tuck under itself so that it rests on the lip of the pie pan. Decoratively crimp the perimeter using your fingers or a fork.

Cut several ventilation slits in the top crust and glaze with egg wash. Make a few chile-shaped pieces out of pastry scraps, brush them with egg wash then sprinkle with cinnamon. Decorate top of pie with them.

Place a cookie sheet or piece of aluminum foil on the bottom of the oven to catch any juices that may drip.

Put the pie in the center of the preheated oven and bake at 425 degrees for 20 minutes. Reduce temperature to 350 degrees and continue baking approximately 40 to 45 minutes more, or until the top is golden brown and you see juices bubbling through the slits.

If using a glass pyrex pie pan, visually check the bottom of the crust for doneness; it should be brown.

Cover crust edge with pie crust shield or strips of aluminum foil if it begins to burn before pie is done.

Cool on wire rack for one hour.

CHOCOLATE CHESS w/ RED CHILE AND NUTS

*Optional Version with Ginger

Think Fudge Brownie with a KICK!

Makes 1 pie

Pastry for a single crust pie

1/2 cup (1 stick) butter
2 ounces Baker's Semi-Sweet Chocolate Bar or baking chips (60% cacao)
2 eggs, lightly beaten
3/4 cup light brown sugar
1 teaspoon vanilla
1/2 to 1 teaspoon red chile powder*

3/4 cup nuts, toasted and chopped, reserving a few whole ones for decoration (we use walnuts)

Preheat oven to 325 degrees F.

Place butter and chocolate in a small heatproof bowl or pyrex measuring cup. Using a microwave, melt the butter and chocolate in 30 second increments, stirring once or twice with a heatproof spatula or wooden spoon each time until thoroughly mixed. Do not boil. (Double boiler method works, just don't boil the mixture.)

In a small mixing bowl beat the eggs then stir in the brown sugar, mixing until all lumps are gone. Add vanilla and red chile powder to the egg/brown sugar mixture. Mix well.

Stir in melted chocolate and butter. Mix well then beat using a whisk or large fork for at least a minute, incorporating air into mixture. Mixture should almost double in volume. NOTE: You can use an electric mixer but do not overbeat, you'll turn this into a cake instead of a pie. A hand-held egg beater works well.

You can double or triple this recipe easily

Cover the bottom of the unbaked pie crust with nuts, reserving a few whole ones for decoration. Using a spatula, scrape all of the mixture into the pie crust.

Place pie in the center of preheated oven. Bake approximately 35 to 40 minutes. Pie can be a little jiggly in center but if it moves a lot when gently shaken bake a few minutes longer. Cool for one hour.

Note: Pie filling may puff up while baking then fall when cooled, creating cracks, this is ok. Decorate the top with remaining nuts.

*IMPORTANT: Use only pure red chile powder. Do not use a mix that contains other spices. You can start with mild chile powder then try hot for more kick.

Tip: This makes a very thin pie. You may want to double the

recipe and use most of it to fill a pie, reserving the rest in a covered container in the fridge for another use.

We sometimes use the extra filling to make a 'scrap pie.' These are free-form 'pies' utilizing leftover dough scraps, fitted into small individual-size baking pans.

OPTION: CHOCOLATE CHESS W/GINGER

Just eliminate the red chile powder (or not!) and add chopped candied ginger.

OPTION: CHOCOLATE CHESS W/RED CHILE AND CHERRIES, Almonds optional.

You can use a can of cherry pie filling and sprinkle some almonds (optional) or use recipe below:

3 cups frozen cherries
1 cup water
1/2 cup sugar
1 tablespoon cornstarch or tapioca starch

Whisk together starch, sugar and cold water in a medium saucepan. Cook over low heat, stirring until sugar and starch are fully dissolved.

Add cherries and continue to cook until sauce begins to thicken, stirring constantly. You may have to use medium heat but be careful not to scorch.

Let cool about 15 minutes then spoon over cooled pie.

SOUTHWESTERN PEACH w/RED CHILES

It was fall and we were putting up our chiles. While we were bagging them for the freezer our fresh-picked peaches from Utah were delivered. While processing 12 cases of fruit and a few 40-pound sacks of steaming hot roasted chiles, a new pie was born.

Makes 1 pie

Pastry for a double crust pie

6 or 7 peaches, blanched, peeled, pitted and sliced (about 5 cups) OR frozen slices
1/2 cup brown sugar
1/8 to 1/4 cup thickener of choice; tapioca starch, cornstarch or flour (you'll need more if peaches are frozen)
1/4 teaspoon freshly grated nutmeg (optional)

Juice of one lemon
1 tablespoon chopped lemon or orange zest, optional
3/4 cup roasted red chiles, peeled, chopped and drained
Egg white beaten with 1 tablespoon of water, for glaze
Decorative sugar like demerara or crystals (optional)

Preheat oven to 425 degrees F.

Place peach slices in a colander or strainer over larger bowl. Sprinkle with the lemon juice and brown sugar. Mix lightly and set aside. After a few minutes set the peaches aside and add thickener to the liquid in the bowl. Mix well to ensure it dissolves thoroughly.

Gently mix the peaches back into thickened liquid and add the zest and nutmeg, if using. If there is a lot of juice drain some off. Spoon filling into the pastry shell, ensuring that no peach tips are sticking up. Add as many chiles as you dare! Brush the overhanging rim of pastry shell with egg wash.

Lay the top pastry over the peaches, seal edges of both layers of pastry together and crimp. Cut vent holes in top crust. You can opt to cut lattice strips from the top pastry layer and interweave on top of peaches, finishing with a decorative crimp, instead.

Brush top pastry layer with egg wash and sprinkle w/decorative sugar, if desired.

Place pie on center rack of preheated oven and bake approximately 20 minutes, 25 to 30 minutes if peaches are frozen.

If edges of pie crust begin to get too done, cover with aluminum foil strips or a pie crust shield. Reduce temperature to 350 degrees and continue baking approximately 40 to 50 minutes, or until juices are bubbling and crust is nicely browned.

Cool one hour.

'HEARTS ON FIRE' CHERRY w/ RED CHILE POWDER

Even though this contains no cinnamon, it reminds me of Cinnamon Red Hot candies ~ the heart-shaped ones.

Makes 1 pie

Pastry for double crust pie

RECIPE FOR CHEER-Y CHERRY PIE, with additon of
2 to 3 tablespoons of pure red chile powder to taste* OR Fresh or Frozen Red Chiles.

*ALWAYS use pure red chile powder, not a blend of chili spice mix.

Preheat oven to 425 degrees F.

Make cherry pie according to directions, adding red chile powder to dry ingredients. If using hot chile powder, start with less, if using mild chile powder, use more. We use medium chile powder. Alternately, you could use a few fresh or frozen red chiles, roasted, peeled and choppped.

Hint: If you can find a cherry with a stem intact, plop it right in the middle and call it a CHERRY BOMB!

Instead of a traditional top crust, we use a cookie cutter and cut out pastry hearts, overlapping them on the pie in concentric circles.

Apply egg wash and decorative sugar, if using.

Bake according to Cherry Pie recipe.

OLD FASHIONED FAVORITES

Lemon Chess

Pie-O-Neer Pecan-Oat

Coconut Macaroon

Peanut Butter Icebox Pie

LEMON CHESS

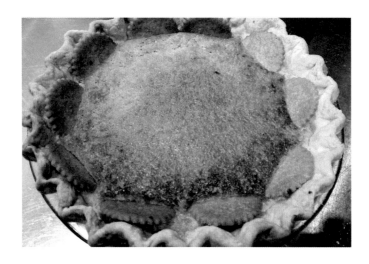

Got Lemons? Make this pie! An especially fun addition is fresh ginger. So pretty adorned with ginger cookies.

Makes 1 pie

Pastry for single crust pie

1 1/2 cups white sugar
2 tablespoons cornmeal, regular or stone ground
1 tablespoon flour
4 eggs
1/4 cup butter, melted
1/4 cup milk
1/4 cup fresh squeezed lemon juice
1 teaspoon vanilla
Zest from 2 lemons
*OPTIONAL: 2 tablespoons fresh grated ginger
*OPTIONAL: Ginger thin cookies for decoration

Preheat oven to 350 degrees F.

In a large bowl stir together sugar, flour and cornmeal.

Add the eggs, butter, milk, vanilla, lemon juice and lemon zest.

*Add the ginger, if using.

Beat with rotary or electric beater until smooth and thoroughly blended.

Pour into pie shell.

*If using ginger thin cookies, line them around edge of pie crust.

Place pie on center rack of preheated oven and bake at 350 degrees for 40 minutes or until set in center and lightly browned.

Cool one hour. Refrigerate leftover pie, loosely covered.

Note: This bold-flavored sweet filling was originally designed for tarts, so the pie should be somewhat shallow. The original recipe calls for more sugar but we've opted for less, adding vanilla to compensate.

PIE-O-NEER PECAN-OAT

*Our most requested recipe, probably because we cut
the sugar so it tastes like a healthy pecan pie!*

Makes 2 pies (freeze one for later, you'll be glad!)

2 unbaked pie shells

1/2 cup butter (1 stick) softened
1/2 cup sugar
1/2 teaspoon salt
1/2 teaspoon cinnamon
1/4 teaspoon ground cloves
1 cup light corn syrup*
1 cup dark corn syrup*
6 eggs
1 cup old-fashioned oats
2 cups pecan pieces, toasted and cooled

12 pecan halves, for decorating

* You can use all light or dark syrup.

Preheat oven to 350 degrees F.

In a large bowl or in the bowl of an electric mixer, cream the butter and sugar together until soft and fluffy. Add salt, cinnamon and cloves. Mix well.

Add syrups and mix well, scraping the sides of bowl as you go.

One at a time, gently blend in eggs. Do NOT whip. If you incorporate too much air at this point your pie will turn into a cake.

Gently stir in the oats. Do not overmix.

Cover each pie crust bottom with a cup of toasted pecan pieces.

Pour mixture evenly into both pie crusts and decorate with pecan halves, placing one on each slice.

Place pies on center rack of preheated oven and bake for 45 to 50 minutes. About halfway through, check to see if pie crust is getting too done around edges. If so, cover pie crust edges with aluminum foil or pie crust shields.

Pies can be a little jiggly in the center when done but tops should be golden brown. If not, continue to bake a few more minutes.

Cool for one hour.

When second pie is completely cool, wrap in plastic then aluminum foil and freeze. When ready to use, unwrap, defrost and reheat in a low oven (250 degrees) for approximately 20 minutes.

COCONUT MACAROON with or without Chocolate

If you like the cookies, you'll love the pie!

Makes 1 pie

Pastry for single crust pie

3/4 cup sugar
1/4 cup flour
1/8 teaspoon salt
2 eggs
1/2 cup (1 stick) butter, melted
1/2 cup water
1 teaspoon vanilla
1 cup flaked coconut, raw, unsweetened

Preheat oven to 350 degrees F.

If you like you can toast some or all of the coconut in the oven while it's preheating. Careful not to burn it.

In a medium bowl mix together sugar, flour, and salt.

In another bowl, beat the eggs then add the butter, water and vanilla. Stir to incorporate.

Whisk dry ingredients into wet ingredients. Add coconut. Stir gently to incorporate.

Pour mixture into pastry shell.

Place pie on center rack of preheated oven. Bake for 35 to 40 minutes or until golden brown on top and set in center.

IF USING CHOCOLATE: Sprinkle chocolate chips or nibs on top of pie while still warm. Once melted, gently spread using a spatula.

Cool one hour.

PEANUT BUTTER ICEBOX PIE

Peanut butter. Cream cheese. Heavy cream. I love those words. Just a hint of sweetness from the powdered sugar seals the deal. Mounded into a crunchy crust of graham crackers and covered with salty peanuts. Heaven!

Makes 1 pie

One Graham Cracker crust (recipe below)

1 sleeve graham crackers, crushed (1-1/4 cups)
1/4 cup sugar
4 tablespoons butter, melted

In a small bowl, mix together crumbs, sugar and butter. Press mixture into a 9" pie pan. Put in freezer to chill well before filling, or bake at 300 degrees for 15 minutes. Cool before using.

FILLING:

8 ounces cream cheese, softened
3/4 cup powdered sugar
3/4 cup peanut butter, crunchy
6 tablespoons milk
1 cup heavy whipping cream
1/2 cup salted peanuts, for garnish

While assembling ingredients, place mixer bowl and beaters in refrigerator for a few minutes. Using electric mixer on medium speed, whip heavy cream until thick, but do not allow to curdle; this can happen quickly. Transfer whipped cream to another bowl, cover and refrigerate. Using same mixer bowl (no need to wash) on lowest speed, mix together cream cheese, powdered sugar and peanut butter. Stop occasionally and scrape down sides of bowl with spatula. Slowly add milk, scraping down sides of bowl as needed, and beat on low just a minute or two more. By hand, gently fold in whipped heavy cream. Spoon mixture into graham crust, spreading carefully - you do not want to pull crust away from pan - and refrigerate several hours or overnight. Garnish with peanuts just before serving. Refrigerate leftovers.

FRUIT

Traditional 2-Crust Apple/Sugar-Free Option

Apple Cranberry Crumb

Junebug's Apple Crumble

Cheer-y-Cherry

Starry-Starry Blueberry Night

Very Berry

Strawberry-Rhubarb

Abiquiu Apricot

French Pear w/Ginger

TRADITIONAL 2-CRUST APPLE
and Sugar-Free Option

What could be more American?

Want a **sugar-free** *version? Use all sweet apples and a pinch more cinnamon.*

Makes 1 pie

Pastry for double crust pie

7 to 8 medium apples, peeled, cored and sliced; we use a   mix of half Granny Smith tart and half sweet apples (any variety except Red Delicious)
1/2 to 3/4 cup sugar (to taste)
2 tablespoons cornstarch
1 to 2 tablespoons cinnamon (to taste)
2 tablespoons lemon juice
2 tablespoons butter, cut into small pieces
Egg wash (1 egg white mixed w/1 tablespoon of water)
Decorative sugar, like demerara or crystals, if desired

Preheat oven to 425 degrees F.

Place apple slices into a large bowl. Sprinkle with sugar, cornstarch and cinnamon. Mix to coat. Add lemon juice. Mix gently.

Spoon apples into bottom of pastry shell. Mound slightly in center. Dot with butter.

Arrange top pastry over apples and seal both top and bottom edges of pastry together. Crimp edges decoratively.

Cut steam vents in top crust. Brush top with egg wash. Sprinkle on decorative sugar, if using. Skip the sugar if making sugar-free version, use cinnamon, instead.

Place in center of preheated oven and bake for approximately 20 minutes.

Reduce temperature to 325 degrees and continue baking another 40 to 50 minutes until juices begin to bubble and top is golden brown.

Check halfway through to make sure crust edges are not burning. If so, cover them with strips of aluminum foil or a pie crust shield.

Cool one hour.

APPLE CRANBERRY CRUMB

The wholesome granola-like topping is sweet and crunchy; the addition of juicy tart cranberries makes the sweet-tart taste POP!

Makes 1 pie

Pastry for single crust pie

7 to 8 medium apples, peeled, cored and sliced; mix of tart Granny Smith and any sweet variety (except Red Delicious)
1/2 cup sugar
2 tablespoons cornstarch
1 to 2 tablespoons cinnamon (to taste)
2 tablespoons lemon juice
3/4 cup fresh or frozen cranberries

CRUMB TOPPING

1/2 cup light brown sugar

1/3 cup flour
1/4 cup butter
1/4 cup old-fashioned oats (not quick cooking)

Preheat oven to 425 degrees F.

Place apple slices in a medium bowl. Toss with sugar, cornstarch, cinnamon and lemon juice. Add cranberries, mix gently and set aside.

While apples are macerating, prepare topping.

To Make the Crumb Topping:

Mix brown sugar and flour in a small bowl. Using a pastry blender or your fingers, cut in butter until mixture resembles large coarse crumbs. Do not overmix or you'll melt the butter. Add oats and mix gently. Set aside.

Fill pastry shell with apple-cranberry mix, mounding slightly in center. If apple tips are sticking up, rearrange slices so that they lay flat. Sprinkle topping over apples, covering the entire surface.

Bake in preheated oven for 20 minutes. Cover pastry edges with pie crust shield or strips of aluminum foil if they start to get too brown.

Reduce temperature to 350 degrees and finish baking approximately 40-45 minutes, or until you see bubbles at edges and topping is golden brown.

Cool on wire rack one hour.

JUNEBUG'S APPLE CRUMBLE

Junebug was a summer helper. One of her tasks was to peel apples and she was determined to become EFFICIENT. It was a proud day when she peeled an entire apple without stopping, producing a long strip of continuous peel as proof. This is her favorite pie.

Makes 1 pie

Pastry for a single crust pie

7 to 8 medium apples, peeled, cored and sliced; half Granny Smith tart, half sweet apples (any kind except Red Delicious)
1/2 cup sugar
2 tablespoons cornstarch
1 to 2 tablespoons cinnamon (to taste)
2 tablespoons lemon juice

TOPPING

1/2 cup light brown sugar
1/3 cup flour
1/4 cup butter
1/4 cup old-fashioned oats (not quick cooking)

Preheat oven to 425 degrees F.

Place apple slices in medium bowl. Toss with sugar, cornstarch, cinnamon and lemon juice. Mix gently and set aside.

Make the Topping:

In a medium bowl, mix brown sugar and flour. Cut in butter with a pastry blender or your fingers. Do not overmix or you will melt the butter. Add oats, mix, set aside.

Pour apples into pie crust, making sure no tips are sticking up. Sprinkle topping over apples, completely covering them.

Bake on the center rack of a preheated oven for about 20 minutes. Cover edges of pastry with strips of aluminum foil or use a pie crust shield if they are beginning to burn.

Reduce temperature to 350 degrees and continue baking for another 40 to 45 minutes, or until juices are beginning to bubble around edges and topping is golden brown.

Cool one hour.

JUNEBUG demonstrates her apple peeling skills

CHEER-Y CHERRY

Yep, you read that right. The bright red color will make you CHEER-Y!

Makes 1 pie

Pastry for a double crust pie

4 1/2 to 5 cups of cherries, pitted (fresh or frozen)
*we use a combination of tart and sweet
1/2 to 3/4 cup sugar (depending on taste)
1/4 cup cornstarch or thickener of your choice
Splash of lemon juice
Egg white mixed with 1 tablespoon of water for glaze
Decorative sugar like demerara or crystals (Optional)

Preheat oven to 425 degrees F.

Put cherries in a medium bowl and splash with a little lemon juice.

In a small bowl mix together sugar and cornstarch.

Sprinkle the sugar/cornstarch mixture over cherries and toss or stir gently to coat. Let stand a few minutes. If excess juice forms in bottom of the bowl of cherries, drain some off. Pour cherries into pastry shell.

Use the other layer of pastry to make a 2-crust pie or make lattice strips or cookie cutouts in shapes of hearts.

Top the cherries with the pastry design of your choice.

If you are making a 2-crust pie: using a pastry brush, glaze the outer rim of the bottom pastry layer with the egg wash mixture. Place the top pastry layer over the cherries. Trim the overhanging top pastry layer to slightly longer length than the bottom layer. Gently press the two layers together to make a seal all around the perimeter of the pie. Lift the overhanging edge of the sealed pastry up slightly and tuck under itself so that it rests on the lip of the pie pan. Decoratively crimp the perimeter using your fingers or a fork. Cut vent holes in top of pastry.

If you are using heart cutouts or strips of lattice, decoratively crimp edges of bottom crust.

Brush pastry with egg wash and sprinkle with decorative sugar, if desired.

Place on center rack of preheated oven and bake approximately 20 minutes. If the edges of the pie crust are starting to burn, cover with strips of aluminum foil or a pie crust shield.

Reduce temperature to 350 degrees and continue baking another 40 to 50 minutes, or until juices are bubbling and top is golden brown.

Cool for one hour.

STARRY-STARRY BLUEBERRY NIGHT

In honor of our dark night skies we top this pie with stars made from pie crust. When it starts to bubble, the stars move up and down, as if twinkling.

Makes 1 pie

Pastry for a double crust pie

4 1/2 to 5 cups of blueberries (fresh or frozen)
1/2 to 3/4 cup sugar (depending on taste)
1/4 cup cornstarch or thickener of your choice
Splash of lemon juice
Egg white mixed with 1 tablespoon of water for glaze
Decorative sugar like demerara or crystals (Optional)

Preheat oven to 425 degrees F.

Put blueberries in a medium bowl and splash with a little lemon juice.

In a small bowl mix together sugar and cornstarch.

Sprinkle the sugar/cornstarch mixture over blueberries and toss or stir gently to coat. Let stand a few minutes. If excess juice forms in bottom of the bowl of blueberries, drain some off. Pour blueberries into pastry shell.

Use the other layer of pastry to make a 2-crust pie or cookie cutouts in shapes of stars.

If making a 2-crust pie: using a pastry brush, glaze the outer rim of the bottom pastry layer with the egg wash mixture. Place the top pastry layer over the blueberries. Trim the overhanging top pastry layer to slightly longer length than the bottom layer. Gently press the two layers together to make a seal all around the perimeter of the pie. Lift the overhanging edge of the sealed pastry up slightly and tuck under itself so that it rests on the lip of the pie pan. Decoratively crimp the perimeter using your fingers or a fork. Cut vent holes in top of pastry.

If using star cutouts, decoratively crimp edge of bottom crust.

Brush pastry with egg wash and sprinkle with decorative sugar, if desired.

Place on center rack of preheated oven and bake approximately 20 minutes. If the edges of the pie crust are starting to burn, cover with strips of aluminum foil or a pie crust shield.

Reduce temperature to 350 degrees and continue baking another 40 to 50 minutes, or until juices are bubbling and top is golden brown.

Cool for one hour.

VERY BERRY

A mulit-colored feast including any berries you like.

Makes 1 pie

Pastry for a double crust pie

4 1/2 to 5 cups of berries, (fresh or frozen) we use sweet & tart cherries, blueberries, raspberries, and blackberries
1/2 to 3/4 cup sugar (depending on taste)
1/4 cup cornstarch or thickener of your choice
Splash of lemon juice
Egg white mixed with 1 tablespoon of water for glaze
Decorative sugar like demerara or crystals (Optional)

Preheat oven to 425 degrees F.

Put berries in a medium bowl and splash with a little lemon juice.

In a small bowl mix together sugar and cornstarch.

Sprinkle the sugar/cornstarch mixture over berries and toss or stir gently to coat. Let stand a few minutes. If excess juice forms in bottom of the bowl of berries, drain some off.

Pour berries into pastry shell.

Use the other layer of pastry to make a 2-crust pie, or make lattice strips, interweaving on top of berries.

If making a 2-crust pie: Using a pastry brush, glaze the outer rim of the bottom pastry layer with the egg wash mixture. Place the top pastry layer over the berries. Trim the overhanging top pastry layer to slightly longer length than the bottom layer. Gently press the two layers together to make a seal all around the perimeter of the pie. Lift the overhanging edge of the sealed pastry up slightly and tuck under itself so that it rests on the lip of the pie pan. Decoratively crimp the perimeter using your fingers or a fork. Cut vent holes in top pastry.

If making lattice top, criss-cross strips of pastry over berries, trimming ends to just over edge of pie pan. With your fingers, roll the bottom pastry overhang up onto rim of pie pan, incorporating strips into it. Decoratively crimp edges.

Brush with egg wash and sprinkle with decorative sugar, if desired.

Place on center rack of preheated oven and bake approximately 20 minutes. If the edges of the pie crust are starting to burn, cover with strips of aluminum foil or use a pie crust shield.

Reduce temperature to 350 degrees and continue baking another 40 to 50 minutes, or until juices are bubbling and top is golden brown.

Cool for one hour.

STRAWBERRY-RHUBARB

The taste and the color are like no other. After Pop McKee passed on, Kathy Elliott grew the best rhubarb in town, this is her recipe.

Makes 1 pie

Pastry for a double crust pie

4 cups strawberries, hulled and sliced (fresh or frozen)
2 to 2 1/2 cups sliced rhubarb (fresh or frozen)
1/2 to 3/4 cup sugar (depending on taste)
3 tablespoons cornstarch or thickener of your choice
Splash of lemon juice
Zest from lemon
2 tablespoons strawberry jam or orange marmalade
Egg white mixed with a tablespoon of water for glaze
Decorative sugar like demerara or crystals (Optional)

Preheat oven to 425 degrees F.

Put strawberries and rhubarb in a medium bowl and splash with lemon juice. Add lemon zest.

In a small bowl mix together sugar and cornstarch.

Sprinkle the sugar/cornstarch mixture over fruit and toss or stir gently to coat. Let stand a few minutes. If excess juice forms in bottom of the bowl of fruit, drain some off before pouring into pastry shell.

Spread jam or marmalade over bottom of pastry shell.

Pour fruit into pastry shell.

Use the other layer of pastry to make a 2-crust pie, or make a lattice topping, interweaving strips of pastry over fruit.

If making a 2-crust pie: Using a pastry brush, glaze the outer rim of the bottom pastry layer with the egg wash mixture. Place the top pastry layer over the fruit. Trim the overhanging top pastry layer to slightly longer length than the bottom layer. Gently press the two layers together to make a seal all around the perimeter of the pie. Lift the overhanging edge of the sealed pastry up slightly and tuck under itself so that it rests on the lip of the pie pan. Decoratively crimp the perimeter using your fingers or a fork.

If making a lattice-top, criss-cross pieces of pastry over fruit, trimming ends to just over edge of pie pan. Using your fingers, roll bottom pastry overhang up onto rim of pie pan, incorporating ends of lattice strips into it. Decoratively crimp edges.

Brush pastry with egg wash and sprinkle with decorative sugar, if desired.

Place on center rack of preheated oven and bake approximately 20 minutes. If the edges of the pie crust are starting to burn, cover with strips of aluminum foil or use a pie crust shield.

Reduce temperature to 350 degrees and continue baking another 40 to 50 minutes, or until juices are bubbling and top is golden brown. Cool for one hour.

For **Rhubarb** freaks: omit strawberries, add more sugar!

Slices of Rhubarb Pie

Alternate top crust using a cut-out stamp

ABIQUIU APRICOT

A stranger brought me a case of freshly picked apricots from Abiquiu. Although I had never made a fresh apricot pie they were so beautiful I had to try. That pie was amazing ~ the color of sunset ~ and that stranger has since become a dear friend.

Makes 1 pie

Pastry for a double crust pie

4 1/2 to 5 cups of sliced apricots, (fresh or frozen)
1/2 to 3/4 cup sugar (depending on taste)
3 tablespoons cornstarch or thickener of your choice
1/2 teaspoon of cinnamon or nutmeg
Splash of lemon juice

Egg white mixed with 1 tablespoon of water for glaze
Decorative sugar like demerara or crystals (Optional)

Preheat oven to 425 degrees F.

Put apricot slices in a medium bowl and splash with lemon juice.

In a small bowl mix together sugar, cornstarch and spice.

Sprinkle the sugar/starch/spice mixture over apricots and toss or stir gently to coat. Let stand a few minutes.

Pour apricots into pastry shell.

Use the other layer of pastry to make a 2-crust pie. Using a pastry brush, glaze the outer rim of the bottom pastry layer with the egg wash mixture. Place the top pastry layer over the apricots. Trim the overhanging top pastry layer to slightly longer length than the bottom layer. Gently press the two layers together to make a seal all around the perimeter of the pie. Lift the overhanging edge of the sealed pastry up slightly and tuck under itself so that it rests on the lip of the pie pan. Decoratively crimp the perimeter using your fingers or a fork. Cut vent holes in top pastry.

Brush with egg wash and sprinkle with decorative sugar, if desired.

Place on center rack of preheated oven and bake approximately 20 minutes. If the edges of the pie crust are starting to burn, cover with strips of aluminum foil or use a pie crust shield.

Reduce temperature to 350 degrees and continue baking another 40 to 50 minutes, or until juices are bubbling and top is golden brown. Cool for one hour.

FRENCH PEAR w/GINGER

Adapted from the Farm Journal Complete Pie Cookbook, my go-to reference manual for pies. A cookie crumb layer of ginger snaps keeps the bottom from becoming soggy. Fresh ginger adds warmth. The finely textured crumb topping is sweet and crisp. Go the extra mile and whip some heavy cream to adorn this delicacy. Oui, oui!

Makes 1 pie

Pastry for a single crust pie

6 or 7 pears, peeled, cored and sliced (about 5 cups)
Medium thumb of fresh ginger, peeled and grated or finely chopped
2 tablespoons lemon juice
Zest of one lemon
Few drops of orange oil or 2 tablespoons orange marmalade
10 to 12 ginger snap cookies, crushed or broken

TOPPING

3/4 cup flour
1/2 cup sugar
1/2 teaspoon cinnamon
1/4 teaspoon salt
1/3 cup butter

Preheat oven to 425 degrees F.

Gently toss pears with ginger, lemon juice, zest and orange oil or marmalade. Set aside.

Spread cookie crumbs/pieces in the bottom of the pastry shell and/or line sides of pie crust. Drain excess juice from pears then place slices in pastry shell, arranging pears so that no tips are sticking up.

In a small bowl mix the flour, sugar, cinnamon and salt. Using a pastry blender or your fingers, cut butter into dry ingredients, mixing well. Sprinkle topping mix on pears, covering the entire surface.

Place pie on center rack of preheated oven and bake approximately 20 minutes. If edges of pie crust are starting to burn, cover with pie crust shield or strips of aluminum foil.

Reduce temperature to 350 degrees and continue baking approximately 40 minutes or until juices start to bubble and topping is lightly browned.

Cool on a wire rack for about an hour.

CREAM PIES & MERINGUES

Gramma Rosie's Coconut Cream

'Sex on a Plate' Chocolate Cream

Banana Cream

Black Bottom Banana Cream

Strawberries and Cream

Peaches and Cream

Stanley's Luscious Lemon Meringue

GRAMMA ROSIE'S COCONUT CREAM w/MERINGUE

Awarded one of the 'Best Pies in the West'
~ Sunset Magazine 2011

Makes 1 pie

1 prebaked pie crust

1/2 cup sugar
3 tablespoons flour
3 tablespoons cornstarch
Pinch salt
1 tablespoon vanilla
4 egg yolks (save whites for meringue)
2 1/4 cup milk (use whole milk)
Mixture of 1/2 cup toasted shredded coconut and 1/2 cup toasted flaked coconut (can use 1 cup of either)

Preheat oven to 275 degrees F.

FILLING

Separate egg yolks from egg whites, putting yolks into a 2-cup pyrex measuring cup (or similar heat proof vessel). Make certain no yolks get into the whites. Reserve the whites in a separate container to be used for meringue.

Mix flour, cornstarch, sugar and salt together in a heavy bottom sauce pan (about 2 quart capacity). Using a wire whisk, stir the milk into the dry ingredients, mixing well. Over medium heat, bring mixture to a simmer while stirring constantly, making certain to scrape bottom and edges of pan on regular intervals. Once mixture begins to simmer, turn the heat to low and put a lid on the pan to keep the mixture hot without allowing bottom to scorch.

Pour almost half of the hot mixture from the pan into the pyrex measuring cup containing the egg yolks while whisking briskly. This will temper the yolks without cooking them. Pour the yolk and milk mixture from the measuring cup back into the pan, whisking to incorporate. Increase heat and slowly bring to a boil, stirring or whisking constantly.

When mixture is bubbling and thickened, add vanilla and remaining 3/4 cup of coconut. Stir well, remove from heat and cover, keeping mixture hot.

At this point, start making meringue.

MERINGUE TOPPING

4 egg whites (reserved from above)
1/3 cup sugar

1/4 teaspoon cream of tartar

In electric mixer bowl, whip sugar on high speed for a minute or two to make it super fine. Add cream of tartar and mix a minute more. With mixer running on medium speed, slowly add egg whites. After a minute or so, turn off mixer and scrape sides and bottom of mixer bowl to ensure sugar is being incorporated into egg whites. Continue to mix a few minutes more until meringue makes peaks when beater is taken out. Do not overmix. Meringue should be shiny and soft.

FILLING (continued)

Pour the hot cream mixture into the cooled pre-baked pie crust containing scattering of coconut. Immediately spread meringue on top of the hot cream making sure to seal meringue against pie crust edges with a spatula. Using a spatula or the back of a large spoon, gently pat down the meringue. As you bring spatula or spoon back up out of meringue you can make decorative peaks. If desired, lightly sprinkle some untoasted coconut over top of meringue for garnish.

Meringue 'Swans'

Place in center of preheated oven and bake at 275 degrees for approximately 25 minutes or until peaks are nicely browned.

Cool at least 30 minutes.

Hint for cutting: Use a lubricant on your knife; dip your knife in water or an unflavored oil like vegetable oil. The slices will come out perfectly!

Leftover pie must be covered and refrigerated.

'SEX ON A PLATE' CHOCOLATE CREAM

Voted 'Best Chocolate Dessert' ~ NM Magazine ~2015 ~ We're crediting the name to Tony Shannon, who liked to lick the plate. Mmmm Good!

Makes 1 pie

1 prebaked pie crust (recipe on separate page)

1/2 cup sugar
3 tablespoons flour
3 tablespoons cornstarch
Pinch salt
1 tablespoon vanilla

4 egg yolks (save whites for meringue)
2 1/4 cup milk (use whole milk)
6 ounces Ghirardelli 60% Cacao Baking Chocolate or similar good quality chocolate, either bar or chips, plus extra for garnish

Preheat oven to 275 degrees F.

FILLING

Separate egg yolks from egg whites, putting yolks into a 2-cup pyrex measuring cup (or similar heat proof vessel). Make certain no yolks get into the whites. Reserve the whites in a separate container to be used for meringue.

Mix flour, cornstarch, sugar and salt together in a heavy bottom sauce pan (about 2 quart capacity). Using a wire whisk, stir the milk into the dry ingredients, mixing well. Over medium heat, bring mixture to a simmer while stirring constantly, making certain to scrape bottom and edges of pan on regular intervals. Once mixture begins to simmer, turn the heat to low and put a lid on pan to keep the mixture hot without allowing bottom to scorch.

Pour almost half of the hot mixture from the pan into the pyrex measuring cup containing the egg yolks while whisking briskly. This will temper the yolks without cooking them.

Pour the yolk and milk mixture from the measuring cup back into the pan, whisking to incorporate. Increase heat and slowly bring to a boil, stirring or whisking constantly.

When mixture is bubbling and thickened, add vanilla and chocolate, stirring to dissolve chocolate. Remove from heat and cover, keeping mixture hot.

At this point, start making meringue.

MERINGUE TOPPING

4 egg whites (reserved from above)
1/3 cup sugar
1/4 teaspoon cream of tartar

In electic mixer bowl, whip sugar on high speed for a minute or two to make it super fine. Add cream of tartar and mix a minute more.

With mixer running on medium speed, slowly add egg whites. After a minute or so, turn off mixer and scrape sides and bottom of mixer bowl to ensure sugar is being incorporated into egg whites. Continue to mix a few minutes more until meringue makes peaks when beater is taken out. Do not overmix. Meringue should be shiny and soft.

FILLING (continued)

Pour the hot cream mixture into a cooled prebaked pie crust.

Immediately spread meringue on top of the hot cream making sure to seal meringue against pie crust edges with a spatula. Using a spatula or the back of a large spoon, gently pat down the meringue. As you bring spatula or spoon back up out of meringue you can make decorative peaks. Garnish with shaved chocolate or chips, if desired.

Place on center rack of preheated oven and bake at 275 degrees for approximately 20 to 25 minutes or until peaks are nicely browned.

Cool at least 30 minutes, preferably an hour.

Hint for cutting: Use a lubricant on your knife; dip your knife in water or an unflavored oil like vegetable oil. The slices will come out perfectly!

Leftover pie must be covered and refrigerated.

BANANA CREAM

Both of my parents grew up eating this classic treat so it was on our table often. It reminds me of banana pudding, like comfort food in a crust.

Makes 1 pie

1 prebaked pie crust (see directions on separate page)

1/2 cup sugar
3 tablespoons flour
3 tablespoons cornstarch
Pinch salt
1 tablespoon vanilla
4 egg yolks (save whites for meringue)
2 1/4 cup milk (use whole milk)
2 to 3 ripe bananas, cut into thick slices or small chunks

Preheat oven to 275 degrees F.

FILLING

Separate egg yolks from egg whites, putting yolks into a 2-cup pyrex measuring cup (or similar heat proof vessel). Make certain no yolks get into the whites. Reserve the whites in a separate container to be used for meringue.

Mix flour, cornstarch, sugar and salt together in a heavy bottom sauce pan (about 2 quart capacity). Using a wire whisk, stir the milk into the dry ingredients, mixing well. Over medium heat, bring mixture to a simmer while stirring constantly, making certain to scrape bottom and edges of pan on regular intervals. Once mixture begins to simmer turn the heat to low and put a lid on the pan to keep the mixture hot without allowing bottom to scorch.

Pour almost half of the hot mixture from the pan into the pyrex measuring cup containing the egg yolks while whisking briskly. This will temper the yolks without cooking them.

Pour the yolk and milk mixture from the measuring cup back into the pan, whisking to incorporate. Increase heat and slowly bring to a boil, stirring or whisking constantly.

When mixture is bubbling and thickened, add vanilla. Stir well, remove from heat and cover, keeping mixture hot.

At this point, start making meringue.

MERINGUE TOPPING

4 egg whites (reserved from above)
1/3 cup sugar
1/4 teaspoon cream of tartar

In electric mixer bowl, whip sugar on high speed for a minute or two to make it super fine. Add cream of tartar and mix a minute more.

With mixer running on medium speed, slowly add whites. After a minute or so, turn off mixer and scrape sides and bottom of mixer bowl to ensure sugar is being incorporated into egg whites. Continue to mix a few minutes more until meringue makes peaks when beater is taken out. Do not overmix. Meringue should be shiny and soft.

FILLING (continued)

Pour about a quarter of the hot cream mixture into a small bowl and let cool a few minutes, while keeping the rest of the cream hot.

Stanley demonstrates cooling technique for cream

Place banana slices or chunks in bottom of cooled prebaked pie crust, covering the bottom. Spoon the slightly cooled cream over the bananas, then add the rest of the hot cream just before topping with meringue. This technique helps keep the bananas from turning mushy and brown.

Ripe but not mushy bananas work well

Immediately spread meringue on top of the hot cream making sure to seal meringue against pie crust edges with a spatula. Using a spatula or the back of a large spoon, gently pat meringue down as you spread it. As you bring the spatula or spoon back up out of meringue you can make decorative peaks.

Place in center of preheated oven and bake at 275 degrees for approximately 25 minutes or until peaks are nicely browned.

Cool at least 30 minutes, preferably an hour.

Hint for cutting: Use a lubricant on your knife; dip your knife in water or an unflavored oil like vegetable oil. The slices will come out perfectly!

Leftover pie must be covered and refrigerated.

BLACK BOTTOM BANANA CREAM

Comfort food taken UP a notch. Slather the bottom of the prebaked pie crust with melted chocolate chips or ganache before you fill it with the bananas and cream.

Makes 1 pie

1 prebaked pie crust (see directions on separtate page)

USE RECIPE FOR BANANA CREAM PIE, with the addition of :

CHOCOLATE GANACHE

*8 ounces Baker's Chocolate, semi-sweet or bittersweet or use good quality baking chips
*2/3 cup heavy cream

*NOTE: Chocolates have varying amounts of cocoa. The higher the percentage, the more cream it will need. Example: 50%

Cocoa, use a 2 to 1 ratio of chocolate to cream; 70% Cocoa, use a 1 to 1 ratio of chocolate to cream.

Chop bars into small pieces (or use baking chips) and place in bottom of heat-proof bowl.

In a heavy bottom saucepan, bring heavy cream to a simmer, stirring occasionally. DO NOT BOIL. As soon as the cream begins to simmer pour it over chocolate pieces, shaking bowl a bit to make sure all pieces are covered. Cover bowl with a lid and let sit undisturbed for about 5 minutes.

Remove lid and whisk. Let sit about 15 minutes, or until it is the consistency to spread. If too thin, put it in the refrigerator for a few minutes or add a bit more melted chocolate. If it is too thick, add a very small amount of warm cream until spreadable. Spread onto bottom of prebaked, cooled pie crust.

Alternate method: Instead of ganache, cover bottom of prebaked pie shell with chocolate baking chips while it is still cooling, so that the chips get slightly melted.

At this point begin making meringue.

MERINGUE TOPPING

4 egg whites (reserved from above)
1/3 cup sugar
1/4 teaspoon cream of tartar

In electric mixer bowl, whip sugar on high speed for a minute or two to make it super fine. Add cream of tartar and mix a minute more.

With mixer running on medium speed, slowly add egg whites. After a minute or so, turn off mixer and scrape sides and bottom of mixer bowl to ensure sugar is being incorporated into egg whites. Continue to mix a few minutes more until meringue makes peaks when beater is taken out. Do not overmix. Meringue should be shiny and soft.

Place banana chunks in pie crust on top of chocolate/ganache.

Using the cream from the BANANA CREAM PIE RECIPE, spread the slightly cooled cream mixture over the bananas to cover, then pour in the rest of the hot cream. Immediately top with meringue.

When spreading meringue make sure to seal topping against pie crust edges with a spatula. Using a spatula or the back of a large spoon, gently pat meringue down as you spread it. As you bring spatula or spoon back up out of meringue you can make decorative peaks.

Place on center rack of preheated oven and bake at 275 degrees for approximately 20 to 25 minutes or until peaks are nicely browned.

Cool at least 30 minutes, preferably an hour.

Hint for cutting: Use a lubricant on your knife; dip your knife in water or an unflavored oil like vegetable oil. The slices will come out perfectly!

Leftover pie must be covered and refrigerated.

STRAWBERRIES & CREAM

All those strawberries, all that cream!!

Makes 1 pie

1 prebaked pie crust (recipe on separate page)

3 tablespoons flour
3 tablespoons cornstarch
1/2 cup sugar
Pinch salt
1 tablespoon vanilla
4 egg yolks
2 1/4 cup milk (use whole milk)

TOPPING

1/2 to 1 pound of strawberries, rinsed, hulled and sliced

3/4 cup of strawberry jam, mixed with enough warm water to make a glaze or make glaze using recipe below

GLAZE

3/4 cup sugar
3 tablespoons cornstarch
1/4 teaspoon salt
1 1/4 cup water
1 cup fruit, chopped
1 teaspoon lemon juice

To prepare glaze:

Combine sugar, cornstarch and salt in heavy-bottom sauce pan. Slowly add water and mix well, making sure no lumps remain. Bring to a boil, stirring constantly. As soon as mixture starts to thicken, reduce heat and add fruit and lemon juice. Continue to stir and cook a few minutes then remove from heat and cool. For a more professional appearance, strain glaze through seive before completely cool.

FILLING

Separate egg yolks from egg whites, putting yolks into a 2-cup pyrex measuring cup (or similar heat proof vessel).

Mix flour, cornstarch, sugar and salt together in a heavy bottom sauce pan (about 2 quart capacity).

Using a wire whisk, stir the milk into the dry ingredients, mixing well. Over medium heat, bring mixture to a simmer while stirring constantly, making certain to scrape bottom and edges of pan on regular intervals. Once mixture begins to simmer, turn the heat to low and put a lid on the pan to keep the mixture hot without allowing bottom to scorch.

Pour almost half of the hot mixture from the pan into the pyrex measuring cup containing the egg yolks while whisking briskly. This will temper the yolks without cooking them. Pour the yolk and milk mixture from the measuring cup back into the pan, whisking to incorporate. Increase heat and slowly bring to a boil, stirring or whisking constantly.

When mixture is bubbling and thickened, add vanilla and stir to mix. Remove from heat and allow to cool a few minutes, stirring a few times to hasten cooling.

Spoon half of glaze in bottom of prebaked pie shell.

When cream is cool but not cold, pour into prebaked pie shell. Place one layer of fruit slices on top of cream, arranging in concentric circles or pattern of your choice. Slices can be overlapping but do not make 2 complete layers. Spoon remaining glaze over fruit and put back in refrigerator for an hour or until cream is set enough to slice.

Leftover pie must be covered and refrigerated.

Lovely served with a dollop of heavy whipped cream!

PEACHES AND CREAM

Summer on a Plate

Makes 1 pie

One prebaked pie crust (recipe on separate page)

3 tablespoons flour
3 tablespoons cornstarch
1/2 cup sugar
Pinch salt
1 tablespoon vanilla
4 egg yolks
2 1/4 cup milk (use whole milk)

TOPPING

5 to 6 peaches, peeled, pitted and sliced (about 5 cups)
3/4 cup of peach jam, mixed with enough warm water to make a glaze or make glaze using recipe below

GLAZE

3/4 cup sugar
3 tablespoons cornstarch
1/4 teaspoon salt
1 1/4 cup water
1 cup fruit, chopped
1 teaspoon lemon juice

To prepare glaze

Combine sugar, cornstarch and salt in heavy-bottom sauce pan. Slowly add water and mix well, making sure no lumps remain. Bring to a boil, stirring constantly. As soon as mixture starts to thicken, reduce heat and add fruit and lemon juice. Continue to stir and cook a few minutes then remove from heat and cool. For a more professional appearance, strain glaze through sieve before completely cool.

FILLING

Separate egg yolks from egg whites, putting yolks into a 2-cup pyrex measuring cup (or similar heat proof vessel). Mix flour, cornstarch, sugar and salt together in a heavy bottom sauce pan (about 2 quart capacity).

Using a wire whisk, stir the milk into the dry ingredients, mixing well. Over medium heat, bring mixture to a simmer while stirring constantly, making certain to scrape bottom and edges of pan on regular intervals. Once mixture begins to simmer, turn the heat to low and put a lid on the pan to keep the mixture hot without allowing bottom to scorch.

Pour almost half of the hot mixture from the pan into the pyrex measuring cup containing the egg yolks while whisking briskly. This will temper the yolks without cooking them. Pour the yolk and milk mixture from the measuring cup back into the pan, whisking to incorporate. Increase heat and slowly bring to a boil, stirring or whisking constantly.

When mixture is bubbling and thickened, add vanilla and stir to mix. Remove from heat and allow to cool a few minutes, stirring a few times to hasten cooling.

Spoon half of glaze in bottom of prebaked pie shell.

When cream is cool but not cold, pour into prebaked pie shell. Place one layer of fruit slices on top of cream, arranging in concentric circles or pattern of your choice. Slices can be overlapping but do not make 2 complete layers. Spoon remaining glaze over fruit and put back in refrigerator for an hour or until cream is set enough to slice.

Leftover pie must be covered and refrigerated.

Lovely served with a dollop of heavy whipped cream!

STANLEY'S LUSCIOUS LEMON MERINGUE

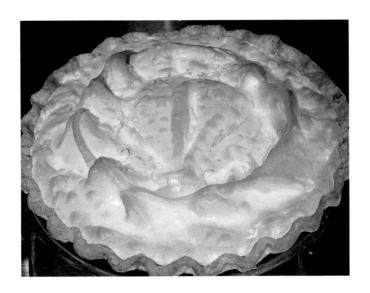

I rescued this recipe from a tattered piece of a cornstarch box my mother used. I reduced the sugar and increased the lemon juice; biting into this confection is like popping a lemon drop in your mouth. I taught my partner how to make it so well that it's now considered 'his' pie. Pretty smart on my part.

Makes 1 pie

One prebaked pie crust (recipe on separate page)
7/8 cup sugar
1/4 cup cornstarch
1 1/4 cup water
1/2 cup fresh squeezed lemon juice
3 egg yolks (reserve whites for meringue)
1 tablespoon butter

Zest from 2 lemons, chopped, 3/4 for filling and 1/4 for top

Preheat oven to 275 degrees F.

In a medium-size heavy-bottom saucepan whisk together sugar and cornstarch.

Add water slowly and whisk well, ensuring dry ingredients do not stick to sides and bottom of pan.

At this point prepare Meringue.

MERINGUE TOPPING

3 egg whites (reserved from above)
1/3 cup sugar
1/4 teaspoon cream of tartar

Put sugar in bowl of an electric mixer. On medium speed, beat the sugar for a minute or two to make it super fine. Add the cream of tartar and beat one minute more. With the mixer still on medium speed, slowly add egg whites and beat on medium speed for a few minutes until the meringue is a consistency that will make small peaks when the beater is lifted out of the meringue.

FILLING (Continued)

Cook mixture over medium heat, stirring constantly until it starts to thicken and begins to look transparent and shiny. Beat in egg yolks and continue stirring until mixture comes to a boil. Add lemon juice and continue stirring until mixture returns to a boil.

Reduce heat but keep mixture simmering while adding the butter and 3/4 of the zest. Continue cooking and stirring approximately one minute. Remove from heat.

Immediately pour hot mixture into cooled, prebaked pie shell. Top hot mixture with meringue. Make certain meringue seals against edges of crust. Using a spatula or the back of a spoon, push down into the meringue and pull back up, creating tips.

Place on center rack of preheated oven and bake for 15 to 20 minutes or until meringue begins to brown. Remove from oven and decorate with remaining lemon zest.

Cool one hour. Refrigerate leftovers, lightly covered with aluminum foil or a dome.

JUST FOR THE FUN OF IT

Plum Ginger Crumb with Candied Walnuts

Coco-Choco-Mac

Chocolate Pecan-Oat

Sweet Potato Pecan-Oat

Customs Upside Down Apple Pecan

Coconut Flan with Optional Chocolate Glaze

PLUM GINGER CRUMB w/ CANDIED WALNUTS

*The WOW factor of the candied walnuts
makes this a great party pie*

Makes 1 pie

Pastry for a single crust pie

6 to 8 plums, pitted and sliced (about 4 1/2 cups)
1/4 cup all-purpose flour
1/4 teaspoon salt
1/4 teaspoon cinnamon
1/4 cup white sugar
1/3 cup brown sugar
1 medium thumb ginger, peeled and chopped (about 2 tablespoons)
1 tablespoon fresh-squeezed lemon juice
Zest of one lemon

Make the candied walnuts before making the pie!

CANDIED WALNUTS (courtesy Allrecipes.com/Dawn's Candied Walnuts)

1 pound walnut halves
1 cup white sugar
2 teaspoons cinnamon
1/4 teaspoon salt
6 tablespoons milk
1 teaspoon vanilla extract

Preheat oven to 350 degrees F.

Spread nuts in a single layer on baking sheet. Roast 8 to 10 minutes or until nuts are golden brown.

In medium bowl, mix together sugar, cinnamon, salt, milk and vanilla. Stir well to make a syrup.

Add toasted walnuts to sugar syrup and stir to coat well. Spoon nuts onto waxed paper and immediately separate with a fork. Cool and store in airtight container until ready to use.

FOR THE PIE

Preheat oven to 425 degrees F.

Place sliced plums into a medium bowl. Sprinkle with lemon juice; add zest and ginger, mix gently and let macerate.

In a small bowl combine flour, salt, cinnamon and both sugars. Sprinkle spice/flour/sugar mixture over plums and gently mix, avoiding breaking up plum slices.

If there is a lot of juice in the bottom of the bowl of plum mixture drain some off before filling pie crust.

Pour plum mixture into prepared pie crust. Sprinkle crumb topping all over plums to cover.

CRUMB TOPPING

1/3 cup flour
1/4 cup white sugar
1/4 cup brown sugar
1/4 teaspoon nutmeg (optional)
1/3 cup old-fashioned oats (not quick cooking)
1/4 cup (1/2 stick) butter, cold and cubed

In a small bowl combine flour, sugars and oats. Using a pastry blender (or your fingers) cut in butter until mixture resembles coarse crumbs. Don't overmix or you'll melt the butter.

Bake at 425 degrees for 15 to 20 minutes.

Reduce temperature to 350 degrees. Sprinkle candied walnuts on top of crumb topping and continue baking for another 40 to 50 minutes until crust is golden brown and filling is bubbling. During this time, watch to make sure your pie crust is not getting too brown; if so, cover perimeter of pie crust with strips of aluminum foil or a pie crust shield.

Let pie cool 30 minutes to an hour. Amazing while still warm with ice cream!

COCO-CHOCO-MAC
with Almonds

*My friend Nita, who baked pies with me in the early days,
came up with this idea after forgetting to put eggs in a
Coconut Macaroon pie. What to do? Put chocolate on top!
All it needed was some almonds and a new pie was born.*

Makes 1 pie

Pastry for single crust pie

3/4 cup sugar
1/4 cup flour
1/8 teaspoon salt
2 eggs
1/2 cup (1 stick) butter, melted
1/2 cup water

1 teaspoon vanilla, or chocolate extract
1 cup flaked coconut, raw and unsweetened
6 oz. Ghirardelli Baker's Chocolate Chips (divided in half)
1 cup almonds, toasted and chopped (divided in half)

Preheat oven to 350 degrees F.

You can toast some or all of the coconut in the oven while it's preheating. Be careful not to burn it.

In a medium bowl mix together sugar, flour, and salt.

In another medium bowl beat the eggs then add the butter and water. Stir to incorporate.

Whisk dry ingredients into wet ingredients. Add coconut. Stir gently to incorporate.

Cover the bottom of the pastry shell with half of the chocolate chips and half of the almonds. Pour mixture into shell.

Place the pie on center rack of a preheated oven and bake for approximately 35 to 40 minutes, or until top is nicely browned and pie is set in center.

As soon as you take the pie out of the oven, sprinkle the rest of the chocolate chips on the top of the hot pie. The chocolate will spread easier if you let it melt for a minute.

Sprinkle top with remaining almond for garnish.

Nita's Coco-Choco-Mac creation

CHOCOLATE PECAN-OAT

The most decadent pie we make ~ it's a good thing we cut the sugar in half!

Makes 1 pie

Pastry for a single crust pie

*Follow the **PIE-O-NEER PECAN-OAT** RECIPE, incorporating:

3 tablespoons cocoa powder or about 6 ounces chocolate baking chips

Add 3 tablespoons cocoa powder to your spices and mix well to incorporate. If using baking chips, add to mix.

*We use 100% cacao powder. If you don't have cacao powder, use

chocolate chips. We use 60% Ghirardelli, but any good quality dark chocolate will do, even bars.

When pies come out of the oven, sprinkle a generous handful of chocolate chips on top and let melt. Spread with knife or spatula to cover pie.

Decorate with pecan halves or pieces on each slice.

CUSTOMS UPSIDE DOWN APPLE PECAN

While clearing Customs in the Houston airport an agent asked me where Pie Town was. "You need to get out of Texas more often," I replied. He then quickly offered me a verbal rendition of the recipe below. He said his mother made the 'Best Apple Pie Ever.' Sir, you may be right!

Makes 1 pie

Pastry for 2 crust pie

7 to 8 medium apples, half Granny Smith, half Fuji or Gala (or any sweet apple except Red Delicious)
1/2 to 3/4 cup sugar, depending on taste
2 tablespoons cornstarch or thickener of choice
1 to 2 tablespoons cinnamon (to taste)
2 tablespoons lemon juice
2 tablespoons butter, softened

Preheat oven to 425 degrees F.

Peel, core and slice apples into a large bowl. Sprinkle with sugar, starch and cinnamon. Mix to coat. Add the lemon juice. Mix gently.

Liberally butter the entire inside surface of a pie pan. Sprinkle pecan pieces to cover bottom. Sprinkle brown sugar evenly over pecan pieces.

Place bottom layer of pastry in pie pan, over pecan pieces and brown sugar. Tap it gently into place in the pan without smashing it down.

Pour apples into pastry shell. Place other layer of pastry on top of apples and seal edges of both layers together. Crimp edges and cut vent holes in top layer of pastry.

Place pie in center of oven and bake at 425 degrees for approximately 20 minutes. Reduce temperature to 350 degrees and continue baking 35 to 40 minutes until juices are bubbling out of vent holes and top is golden brown.

Cool about 30 minutes, then invert the pie onto a cookie sheet, baking pan or a pretty plate. If the pie sticks to pie pan, use a knife to gently loosen. Even if it breaks a little, it's still going to be fabulous!

Cool for an hour and enjoy this taste treat.

SWEET POTATO PECAN-OAT

"Tastes like a holiday in my mouth" ~ CDT Hiker

Makes 1 pie

Pastry for a single crust pie

*Follow the recipe for **Pie-O-Neer Pecan-Oat**; refrigerate mix while baking sweet potatoes.

2 large or 3 small/medium sweet potatoes
1/2 cup heavy cream
Smear of molasses

Preheat oven to 375 degrees F.

To make the SWEET POTATO bottom layer:

Wash and prick holes in sweet potatoes. Arrange in baking dish so they don't touch. Cover with aluminum foil and bake for an hour or until potatoes are soft and look caramelized.

When potatoes are slightly cooled the flesh should easily separate from the peels. Scrape the flesh into a mixing bowl and discard the peels. Mash the potatoes then add heavy cream and mash/whip a little more.

Spread a very thin layer of molasses on bottom of cold, unbaked pie shell. This will act as a moisture shield and impart another flavor profile to the pie.

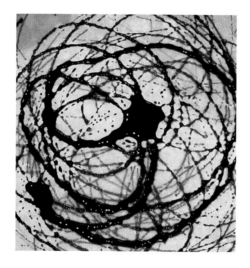

Spread sweet potato/cream mixture on top of molasses.

Place on center rack of preheated oven and bake for approximatley 25 minutes. Take out of oven and place on cooling rack. Filling may have puffed up and will fall.

Sprinkle most of the toasted pecan pieces from the pecan-oat recipe over sweet potato layer.

Pour the pecan-oat mixture in, filling to just under rim of fluted edge of pie crust.

Reduce temperature to 325 degrees and finish baking for another 25 to 30 minutes. Mixture can jiggle a little in center but the top should be golden brown.

Decorate top of pie with remaining pecan pieces.

Cool for one hour.

COCONUT FLAN with Optional Chocolate Glaze

Creaminess of custard with healthy coconut chips.
Chocolate syrup adds a touch of decadence.

1 prebaked pie crust

1 13.5 oz. can unsweetened coconut milk
1 14 oz. can sweetened condensed milk
3 large eggs
1/3 cup water
1 teaspoon vanilla extract
1 cup unsweetened coconut chips or flakes, toasted (reserve some for decorating top)
1 teaspoon coconut extract (optional)

Preheat oven to 350 degrees F.

Combine coconut milk, sweetened condensed milk, eggs, water and vanilla in blender. Blend one minute.

Add most of the coconut, reserving some for top. Add coconut extract, if using. Blend for 30 seconds.

Pour into prebaked pie crust. Bake 50-55 minutes or until knife inserted in center comes out clean.

Cool 30 minutes. Glaze with chocolate syrup, if desired.

Leftovers must be loosely covered and refrigerated.

ACKNOWLEDGEMENTS

This compilation of recipes is only possible because of the many helpers who have shared their piemaking experiences and taught me things I needed to know in order to become a better piemaker. I **THANK** each one of them for their generosity and encouragement. They know who they are, and they know I couldn't have done all of this without them...their special touches are all over these pages.

Pie Festival

What could be more fun than a day dedicated to PIE?

Every 2nd Saturday in September the annual Pie Festival draws thousands of visitors. There's a pie baking contest, a pie eating contest, a Pi-K Run and lots of other activities.

Families gather in the park for a day of fun and then dance to a live band at night. A highlight is the auction of the prize-winning pies!

Quality Control Crew: Kathy, Tanya & Jenny

Pi Day 3.14

Every March 14 (3.14) we celebrate the mathematical equasion Pi.

People come from all over THE WORLD for a piece of pie on Pi Day.

The Pi Day Crew 2018

Rose, Jenny, Joanie, Stanley, Me, Terri, John & Nita

Pie Queens

Every year we nominate a Pie Queen (& King). The reigning
Queen/King receives a tiara and a custom decorated
apron and rolling pin...and bragging rights!

Pie Queens preparing to crown Kathy Elliott in 2017: Nita Larronde, Cathy
Bissey, Ruth Hanrahan, Kathy Knapp, Karen Bingham, Penny Carroll and Joan
Shannon.

Pie Queen Kathy Elliott inducting Jerry & Nelda Rae McPhaul/2018.

2016 was the year for US!

Stanley King & Kathy Knapp

Pie Ladies

Tanya and Jenny

Jenny, me and Megan

Jenny with her 4th of July pie

Pi Bar Brand & Pie Bar

Pie-ateria Trays

STANLEY KING

Stanley King, my partner in **all** things, deserves most of the praise for the sucesss of the Pie-O-Neer. Without his business know-how, engineering background and extensive tool kit I would not have been able to keep the doors swinging. And, he makes the BEST cream pies!

WENDI RAE CARRILLO

Wendi Rae, what can I say? You were there when it was just you and your Granny. Day one. Ground Zero. Whatever she needed, you made it happen. And you learned so much about life in the process.

It was a hard transition when your Grandma had to leave, her absence created such a void. I know it wasn't always easy, but **THANK YOU** for always being there for me while I was fumbling my way through becoming a pie lady.

Granny is proud of you, and so am I.

Yes, we do see things in our pie crust!

This is my first attempt at publishing and I owe a very special **THANK YOU** to Lissa Moore for her keen eyes, practical experience and calm patience while editing. You made this project easier for me Lissa, and much, much better for everyone else.

Everyone at the **Continental Divide Trail Coalition,** especially Teresa Martinez, Executive Director and Co-Founder. Their work has made it possible for the trail to continue being used by all the people who hiked and/or biked the CDT through Pie Town. I was happy to offer a little 'trail magic' and earn the title of 'Trail Angel."

CONTINENTAL TRAIL DIVIDE CREW
Nita, Christy, Teresa, me, Stanley, Lisa & Tom

Continental Divide Trail Logo

Trail Magic

A group of hikers was in the pie shop when a hot-from-the-oven apple cranberry crumb pie slid off the pie rack. The unmistakable sound of a pie hitting the floor got everyone's attention. The pie had landed on the linoleum upside down but remarkably intact. *"PIE DOWN!"* I exclaimed as I went for the broom and dustpan. Several hikers came to my aid, asking if they could *'help.'* I realized what they meant and traded my broom for a bench scraper. We flipped it over and it didn't look that bad. I set the pie in the middle of their table and it was eagerly devoured while still hot. We call this TRAIL MAGIC!

"PIE DOWN!"

DIGGING IN
Kim & Andy Dyer, Lisa Peru, Chilton Tippin & friend

Some Impressive Pie Press

Pie Lady of Pie Town Film

Pie Town Revisited Book

CBS Sunday Morning Show

The Food Network

New Mexico True

Travel & Leisure

Sunset Magazine

Pie Lady of Pie Town Documentary

Jane Rosemont produced and directed a short film about Pie Town in 2014. It is a beautiful story about love, moms and pie. The film has won several awards, including 'Audience Choice Award' after screening for an enthusiastic audience at the Chinese Theater on Hollywood Boulevard.

Jane and I became fast friends during the making of the film. We then made memories of a lifetime while promoting **Pie Lady of Pie Town** together at film festivals.

Pie Town Revisited

copyright 2014 by Arthur Drooker, published
by University of New Mexico Press

Arthur Drooker, author and photographer, came to Pie Town in 2011 to photograph any remaining people and places that had been previously documented by FSA photographer Russell Lee in the 1940s. Arthur returned several times over several years, developing friendships that allowed him to capture a changing Pie Town through his lens. His portraits and images deftly connect Pie Town's past with its present. And he made me a 'Cover Girl!'

CBS Sunday Morning Show

We had the extreme good fortune to be featured on the CBS Sunday Morning Show in 2014. When Bill Geist gave us his seal of approval Pie Town became a *DESTINATION!*

Image Courtesy of YouTube

4:48 · Nov 30, 2014

A delicious slice of life

Bill Geist travels to Pie Town, New Mexico, a town that's all about ... well, pies!

CBS Sunday Morning

ABOUT THE AUTHOR

Kathy R. Knapp

Photo Credit Jane Rosemont

Kathy lives in Pie Town and can often be found enjoying a slice of pie - that she didn't make - at the Pie-O-Neer.

She also spends time in the Gila Wildneress with her partner, Stanley King, who hosts guests at The Silver Creek Inn & Retreat Center located in the historic ghost town of Mogollon, New Mexico.

Sometimes they bake pies together.

PRAISE FOR AUTHOR

"Some 15 years ago, when I was consulting on culinary tourism for the New Mexico Tourism Department, I started hearing about the Pie-O-Neer in Pie Town. After many years' absence, a pie baker had returned to this historic little burg on the Continental Divide. I devised a trip to Arizona just as an excuse to drive through and meet the Pie Lady of Pie Town, Kathy Knapp. Oh my, oh pie, I was delighted with slices of heaven ~ nubbly pecan-oat, French pear scented with ginger, peach melded with red chile, apple paired with green chile and pine nuts. Perhaps even more indelible in my mind, though, than the superb constellation of desserts, was the effervescent Pie Lady herself. This book is a tasty testament to her years in Pie Town, including recipes for her many fabulous creations. Congratulations on picking up this compendium of Kathy's pie-making secrets. Your life will be better for it. Enjoy!"

~Cheryl Alters Jamison, James Beard award-winning cookbook author and pie fanatic

"After 25 years of helping Pie Town, New Mexico live up to its name, Kathy Knapp knows a thing or two about how to make pie that's worth driving cross-country for. This sweet and spicy collection is a testament to her ingenuity and warmth, and the delicious results that happen when baking is rooted in place. The only thing that could possibly be better than this cookbook is eating pie at the Pie-O-Neer itself. For now, I'll content myself with a homemade slice of Southwestern Peach Pie with Red Chiles."

~Kate Lebo, award-winning author and poet

"If pie is your love language and setting a warm homemade pie on the table before family brings you pleasure like nothing else, you need 'Pie Town Pies,' lovingly composed by the woman who brings joy to the world one pie at a time. On these pages Kathy shares the secrets that have made her a living legend, told in her folksy, friendly voice that brings a smile to the heart. You'll want to work your way through all the scrumptious flavors, like New Mexico Apple Pie with Green Chiles and Pine Nuts and Black Bottom Banana Cream. Bake from this Pie Bible and you'll understand why people from all over the world made the pilgrimage to Pie Town, New Mexico to taste her creations."

~Sharon Niederman, Author, New Mexico Farm Table Cookbook

"Kathy Knapp - a.k.a. The Pie Lady - extends her generosity of spirit beyond her beloved pie shop by sharing her recipes and stories from Pie Town. I've been waiting for this book for a long time and now that 'Pie Town Pies' is here it has instantly become my favorite pie cookbook ever."

"I dare you not to drool on the pages of this book."

~Beth M. Howard, author/blogger/pie maker

Made in the USA
Las Vegas, NV
15 November 2022